just for
one

THE AUSTRALIAN
Women's Weekly

contents

Live on your own? If you're someone who loves cooking, you'll love this book; if, on the other hand, you find cooking a solitary meal a tedious chore, I bet this book changes your attitude. From scaled-down recipes to full-size meals meant to be frozen, there's plenty to excite you to cook for yourself, and to prove that eating alone need not be an uninspired event.

Pamela Clark

Food Director

a singular dining experience

If you're the kind of "cook" who makes a bowl of cereal or two-minute noodles for dinner, this book will inspire you to lash out and experiment with the pleasures of cooking and eating well. With a bit of preparation and planning, you can shop and cook for yourself without spending excessive amounts of time or money, plus enjoy the fruits of your labours and live a healthier lifestyle. Make only what you need for one (or perhaps two) meals: avoid monotony by all means, as you'll quickly tire of cooking if you're not enjoying it. Your two best friends in the kitchen should be your freezer and your microwave oven (if you don't already own one, buy a microwave: they're not expensive and, not only do they defrost food in a jiff, they also speed up and simplify many cooking processes). Make soups, stews, curries and casseroles on rainy weekends and freeze them in individual portions. When you purchase meat, fish and poultry, divide, wrap and freeze them in single meal sizes. You can apply this technique to semi-prepared foods, too – quarter a bag of frozen vegies and package them in snap-lock bags; freeze one of the small pizza bases that are sold packaged in pairs; wrap and freeze one or two rashers of bacon or a pair of sausages. Cooked plain white rice or pasta, pulses and lentils, all freeze well, so make enough for four servings and freeze three of them. Keep small cans and jars of soup, pasta sauce, vegetables, baked beans, tuna, salmon and the like in the cupboard. Buy small amounts of many different fruits and vegetables so that you don't have to eat the same thing night after night, nor have so many that they spoil. Keep half a dozen eggs and some cheese in the fridge. Try different combinations of spices or herbs. Grill a white-fish cutlet or poach a chicken breast fillet in the microwave and top it with a simple fresh salsa or salad and a baked potato. Buy a barbecued chicken, discard the skin and bones: use the meat in a tortilla wrap with cheese and avocado; stir-fry it with cooked rice and a few veg; or with a little cream and mushrooms on top of spaghetti. The list goes on and on: just think of your favourite things to eat and reinvent them by downsizing.

snacks &
light meals

antipasto puff pastry tartlet

preparation time 15 minutes
cooking time 25 minutes

per serving 51g total fat
(20.8g saturated fat); 3248kJ
(777 cal); 50.2g carbohydrate;
25.3g protein; 9.3g fibre

tip For best results, use a pizza tray
with holes in the base – this will make
it possible to cook the pastry evenly.

1 tablespoon olive oil
1 clove garlic, crushed
½ small red capsicum (75g),
    chopped coarsely
½ small yellow capsicum (75g),
    chopped coarsely
1 baby zucchini (15g), sliced thinly
1 baby eggplant (60g), sliced thinly
½ small red onion (50g), sliced thickly
25g semi-dried tomatoes
50g baby bocconcini cheese, halved
2 tablespoons finely grated
    parmesan cheese
6 fresh basil leaves
½ sheet ready-rolled puff pastry
1 tablespoon tomato pasta sauce

1 Preheat oven to 200°C/180°C
fan-forced.
2 Combine oil and garlic in medium
bowl. Add capsicums, zucchini, eggplant
and onion; toss gently to coat vegetables
in mixture.
3 Cook vegetables, in batches, on heated
oiled grill plate (or grill or barbecue)
until browned lightly and just tender;
transfer to medium bowl. Add tomatoes,
cheeses and basil; toss gently to combine.
4 Place pastry on oiled oven tray, fold
edges over to form 1cm border. Spread
sauce over pastry; top with vegetable
mixture. Bake about 15 minutes or until
browned lightly. Serve tartlet topped
with olive tapenade, if desired.

spinach, capsicum and fetta pizza

preparation time 10 minutes
cooking time 10 minutes

per serving 20.9g total fat
(11.9g saturated fat); 2458kJ
(588 cal); 64.6g carbohydrate;
32.7g protein; 5.2g fibre

1 large pitta
2 tablespoons bottled tomato
   pasta sauce
½ cup (55g) coarsely grated
   pizza cheese
20g baby spinach leaves
½ small red capsicum (75g),
   sliced thinly
25g fetta cheese, crumbled

1 Preheat oven to 240°C/220°C
fan-forced.
2 Place pitta on oven tray; spread with
sauce then sprinkle with half of the pizza
cheese. Top with spinach, capsicum and
fetta; sprinkle with remaining cheese.
3 Bake about 10 minutes or until cheese
melts and pizza base is crisp.

reuben sandwich

preparation time 5 minutes
cooking time 10 minutes

per serving 29.5g total fat
(14g saturated fat); 2441kJ
(584 cal); 42.1g carbohydrate;
34.1g protein; 7.2g fibre

tip Sandwich can also be cooked
in a heated sandwich press.

2 slices rye bread
4 (60g) thin slices swiss cheese
¼ cup (50g) sauerkraut
50g thinly sliced corned beef
russian dressing
1 tablespoon mayonnaise
½ teaspoon tomato sauce
½ teaspoon horseradish cream
½ teaspoon worcestershire sauce

1 Combine ingredients for russian
dressing in small bowl; mix well.
2 Top one slice of bread with two
slices of cheese then the sauerkraut,
dressing, beef then remaining cheese.
Top with remaining slice of bread.
3 Place sandwich in heated, oiled frying
pan; cook about 5 minutes or until
cheese starts to melt and bread is
browned lightly. Turn sandwich with
a spatula to brown lightly other side.
Serve immediately.

bruschetta caprese

preparation time 10 minutes
cooking time 5 minutes

per serving 19.5g total fat
(6.7g saturated fat); 1689kJ
(404 cal); 38.2g carbohydrate;
16.5g protein; 3.9g fibre

¼ x long loaf turkish bread
10g baby rocket leaves
100g cherry tomatoes, sliced thickly
50g bocconcini cheese, sliced thickly
1 tablespoon finely shredded fresh basil
2 teaspoons olive oil

1 Split turkish bread in half horizontally;
toast both sides.
2 Top each piece with equal amounts
of rocket, tomato, cheese and basil;
drizzle with oil to serve.

lamb and pesto focaccia

preparation time 5 minutes
cooking time 5 minutes

per serving 34.5g total fat
(15.5g saturated fat); 2700kJ
(646 cal); 24.4g carbohydrate;
56.7g protein; 3.6g fibre

10cm-square piece focaccia
1 tablespoon basil pesto
150g thickly sliced roast lamb
¼ cup (25g) shaved parmesan cheese
2 tablespoons drained, sliced
   sun-dried tomatoes

1 Preheat sandwich press. Cut focaccia
in half horizontally.
2 Spread pesto over base of focaccia,
top with lamb, cheese, tomato and
remaining focaccia.
3 Place focaccia in sandwich press
about 5 minutes or until cheese melts
and focaccia is heated through.
4 Slice focaccia diagonally to serve.

chicken laksa

preparation time 10 minutes
cooking time 5 minutes

per serving 32.9g total fat
(22.9g saturated fat); 3018kJ
(722 cal); 57g carbohydrate;
43.7g protein; 2.7g fibre

tip Substitute your favourite noodles
for the egg noodles, if desired.

75g fresh egg noodles
1 tablespoon laksa paste
¾ cup (180ml) light coconut milk
1 cup (250ml) chicken stock
2 teaspoons lime juice
1 teaspoon brown sugar
1 teaspoon fish sauce
2 kaffir lime leaves, torn
1 cup (120g) coarsely chopped
    barbecued chicken
¼ cup (20g) bean sprouts
2 tablespoons loosely packed fresh
    vietnamese mint leaves

1 Place noodles in small heatproof bowl;
cover with boiling water, separate with
fork, drain.
2 Meanwhile, cook paste in lightly oiled
medium saucepan, stirring, until fragrant.
3 Stir in coconut milk, stock, juice,
sugar, sauce and lime leaves; bring to
a boil. Reduce heat; simmer, covered,
3 minutes. Add chicken; stir until laksa
is heated through.
4 Place noodles in serving bowl. Ladle
laksa over noodles; top with sprouts
and mint.

thai-style chicken and pumpkin soup

makes 2 servings
preparation time 10 minutes
cooking time 5 minutes

per serving 39.5g total fat
(25.8g saturated fat); 2479kJ
(593 cal); 24.3g carbohydrate;
33.8g protein; 4.4g fibre

tips The extra portion can be stored
in an airtight container in the freezer
for up to two months.
You can adjust the amount of curry
paste to suit your taste.
Herb scones are a great accompaniment
with this soup.

1½ tablespoons red curry paste
420g can cream of pumpkin soup
400ml can light coconut milk
¾ cup (180ml) chicken stock
1½ cups (200g) coarsely chopped
    barbecued chicken
2 green onions, sliced thinly
2 tablespoons coarsely chopped
    fresh basil

1 Cook curry paste in medium heated
saucepan, stirring, until fragrant. Add
soup, coconut milk and stock; bring
to a boil.
2 Add chicken; reduce heat. Simmer,
stirring, until soup is heated through.
Stir in onion and basil just before serving.

warm gnocchi salad

preparation time 10 minutes
cooking time 10 minutes

per serving 21.4g total fat
(6.6g saturated fat); 1693kJ
(405 cal); 35.5g carbohydrate;
14.5g protein; 4g fibre

tip Substitute balsamic vinegar for the
red wine vinegar, if you prefer.

125g fresh gnocchi
60g char-grilled capsicum in oil
2 teaspoons red wine vinegar
1 clove garlic, crushed
2 tablespoons seeded black olives
80g marinated artichoke hearts,
    drained, quartered
½ small red onion (50g), sliced thinly
2 tablespoons fresh basil leaves
1 tablespoon toasted walnuts

1 Cook gnocchi in medium saucepan of boiling water, uncovered, until they float to the surface and are just tender; drain. Cover to keep warm.
2 Meanwhile, drain capsicum over small jug; reserve 1 tablespoon of the oil. Slice capsicum thinly.
3 Combine reserved oil in screw-top jar with vinegar and garlic; shake dressing well.
4 Combine capsicum and gnocchi in large bowl with olives, artichoke, onion, basil and dressing; toss gently to combine.
5 Serve salad topped with nuts.

beetroot, asparagus and fetta salad

preparation time 10 minutes
cooking time 5 minutes

per serving 42.7g total fat
(11.1g saturated fat); 2052kJ
(491 cal); 9.5g carbohydrate;
15.6g protein; 5.8g fibre

100g asparagus, halved
50g fetta cheese, crumbled
¼ cup loosely packed fresh mint
 leaves, torn
100g canned beetroot wedges, drained
2 tablespoons roasted walnut halves
lemon dressing
1 clove garlic, crushed
1 tablespoon olive oil
2 teaspoons lemon juice

1 Combine ingredients for lemon
dressing in small jug.
2 Boil, steam or microwave asparagus
until just tender; drain.
3 Combine asparagus, cheese,
mint, beetroot, nuts and dressing in
medium bowl.

blt salad

preparation time 5 minutes
cooking time 10 minutes

per serving 20.7g total fat
(7.2g saturated fat); 1258kJ
(301 cal); 6.5g carbohydrate;
21.4g protein; 2.9g fibre

2 bacon rashers (140g)
4 grape tomatoes, halved
100g cos lettuce leaves
2 tablespoons parmesan cheese flakes
mayonnaise dressing
1 tablespoon mayonnaise
2 teaspoons warm water

1 Cook bacon in small frying pan
until crisp; drain on absorbent paper.
Chop coarsely.
2 Combine ingredients for mayonnaise
dressing in small jug until smooth.
3 Combine bacon, tomato, lettuce and
cheese in medium bowl; toss gently.
4 Just before serving, drizzle salad with
mayonnaise dressing.

ham, brie and fig salad with honey mustard dressing

preparation time 10 minutes

per serving 36.2g total fat
(12.1g saturated fat); 1998kJ
(478 cal); 9g carbohydrate;
28.3g protein; 2.7g fibre

50g radicchio lettuce leaves
20g wild rocket
100g thinly sliced leg ham
1 medium fig (60g), quartered
40g blue brie cheese, sliced thinly
honey mustard dressing
1 teaspoon wholegrain mustard
½ teaspoon honey
1 tablespoon olive oil
1 tablespoon lemon juice

1 Place ingredients for honey mustard
dressing in screw-top jar; shake well.
2 Arrange lettuce, rocket, ham, fig
and cheese on serving plate; drizzle
with dressing.

tuna and lemon linguine

makes 2 servings
preparation time 10 minutes
cooking time 10 minutes

per serving 7.1g total fat
(1.2g saturated fat); 1158kJ
(277 cal); 34.4g carbohydrate;
17.4g protein; 2.1g fibre

tip Take remaining portion to work the
next day for a quick, nutritious lunch.

100g linguine
95g can tuna in oil
½ teaspoon finely grated lemon rind
1 teaspoon lemon juice
1 tablespoon coarsely chopped
    fresh flat-leaf parsley
1 clove garlic, crushed

1 Cook pasta in medium saucepan
of boiling water, uncovered, until just
tender; drain.
2 Combine hot pasta with undrained
tuna, rind, juice, parsley and garlic in
large bowl, toss gently.

tuna, avocado and bean salad

preparation time 10 minutes

per serving 24.4g total fat
(5.6g saturated fat); 1935kJ
(463 cal); 14.5g carbohydrate;
30.7g protein; 8.2g fibre

100g canned red kidney beans,
   rinsed, drained
60g cherry tomatoes, halved
¼ cup loosely packed fresh flat-leaf
   parsley leaves
2 tablespoons fresh coriander leaves
½ small red onion (50g), sliced thinly
95g can tuna in oil
1 tablespoon red wine vinegar
½ small avocado (100g)

1 Combine beans, tomato, herbs and onion in medium bowl; toss gently.

2 Drain tuna, reserve 1 tablespoon of the oil. Place reserved tuna oil and vinegar in screw top jar; shake well.

3 Arrange salad and flaked tuna on serving plate. Top with avocado; drizzle with dressing.

tandoori chicken drumettes with cucumber raita

preparation time 5 minutes
cooking time 20 minutes

per serving 21.4g total fat
(6.9g saturated fat); 1413kJ
(338 cal); 6.3g carbohydrate;
28.5g protein; 1.6g fibre

tips Raita is a fresh yogurt salad that
goes very well with spicy Indian dishes.
Chicken drumettes are, in fact, wings
trimmed to resemble drumsticks; in
some areas, this name is used (along
with lovely legs) when describing
pared-back and trimmed drumsticks.
You can use either in this recipe.

2 teaspoons tandoori paste
100g yogurt
3 chicken drumettes (240g)
¼ lebanese cucumber (30g), seeded,
  chopped finely
1 teaspoon finely chopped fresh mint
¼ teaspoon ground cumin

1 Preheat oven to 200°C/180°C
fan-forced.
2 Combine paste and half the yogurt in
large bowl. Add chicken; toss until well
coated. Place chicken, in single layer, on
wire rack over baking dish; roast about
20 minutes or until chicken is browned
all over and cooked through.
3 Combine remaining yogurt with
cucumber, mint and cumin in small
bowl. Serve tandoori chicken topped
with cucumber raita.

warm potato and salmon salad

preparation time 15 minutes
cooking time 15 minutes

per serving 33.1g total fat
(17.7g saturated fat); 2408kJ
(576 cal); 34.3g carbohydrate;
32.2g protein; 5.3g fibre

tip Use tweezers to remove any
bones from the salmon.

250g baby new potatoes
125g salmon fillet
¼ cup (60g) sour cream
1 teaspoon lemon juice
2 teaspoons coarsely chopped
   fresh dill
1 clove garlic, crushed
20g baby spinach leaves

1 Boil, steam or microwave potatoes
until just tender; drain. Slice thickly.
2 Meanwhile, place salmon in medium
frying pan filled with just enough
simmering water to barely cover fish.
Simmer, covered, about 4 minutes or
until salmon is cooked as desired; drain
on absorbent paper.
3 Place sour cream, juice, dill and garlic
in small jug; whisk to combine.
4 Slice salmon; arrange potato, spinach
and salmon on serving plate, drizzle
with dressing.

spaghettini with rocket, pine nuts and sun-dried capsicum

preparation time 10 minutes
cooking time 15 minutes

per serving 48.4g total fat
(6.1g saturated fat); 3829kJ
(916 cal); 93.4g carbohydrate;
24g protein; 5.6g fibre

125g spaghettini
1 tablespoon olive oil
2 tablespoons roasted pine nuts,
    chopped coarsely
1 fresh small red thai chilli, seeded,
    chopped finely
1 clove garlic, crushed
80g sun-dried capsicums, drained,
    chopped coarsely
20g rocket, shredded finely
1 tablespoon coarsely grated
    parmesan cheese

1 Cook pasta in large saucepan of
boiling water, uncovered, until just
tender; drain.
2 Meanwhile, heat oil in medium
saucepan, add pine nuts, chilli and
garlic; cook, stirring, until fragrant. Add
pasta, capsicum and rocket; toss until
rocket is just wilted.
3 Serve pasta sprinkled with cheese.

grills

chicken with capers, anchovies and rosemary

preparation time 10 minutes
cooking time 30 minutes

per serving 40.9g total fat
(13.3g saturated fat); 2370kJ
(567 cal); 0.9g carbohydrate;
49g protein; 0.6g fibre

2 teaspoons drained capers, rinsed,
  chopped finely
1 clove garlic, crushed
2 drained anchovies, chopped finely
1 teaspoon fresh rosemary leaves
2 chicken thighs (400g)

1 Combine capers, garlic, anchovies
and rosemary in small bowl.
2 Preheat grill to hot.
3 Cut two deep slashes into each
chicken thigh. Place a teaspoon of
the caper mixture into each slash.
4 Cook chicken, skin-side down, under
grill about 15 minutes; turn chicken,
cook a further 15 minutes or until
browned and cooked through.
5 Serve chicken with salad leaves and
steamed baby potatoes, if desired.

fish with thai-style dressing

preparation time 10 minutes
cooking time 8 minutes

per serving 1.3g total fat
(0.2g saturated fat); 915kJ
(219 cal); 8.8g carbohydrate;
41.6g protein; 1.2g fibre

25g snow pea shoots, trimmed
¼ cup loosely packed fresh mint leaves
2 tablespoons fresh coriander leaves
1 fresh small red thai chilli, seeded,
   sliced thinly
200g firm white fish fillet
1 tablespoon lime juice
2 teaspoons grated palm sugar
2 teaspoons fish sauce

1 Combine snow pea shoots, mint, coriander and chilli in medium bowl.
2 Cook fish on heated, oiled grill plate (or grill or barbecue) about 4 minutes each side, or until browned and just cooked through.
3 Meanwhile, combine juice, sugar and sauce in small bowl.
4 Serve fish topped with salad and drizzled with lime dressing.

barbecued vegetables and haloumi with lemon basil dressing

preparation time 10 minutes
cooking time 10 minutes

per serving 25.8g total fat
(4.4g saturated fat); 1195kJ
(286 cal); 5.4g carbohydrate;
6.4g protein; 3.2g fibre

50g baby spinach leaves
50g char-grilled red capsicum,
   sliced thickly
50g marinated artichokes, halved
2 tablespoons green olives
1 portobello mushroom
10g haloumi cheese, sliced thickly
lemon basil dressing
2 teaspoons lemon juice
1 tablespoon extra virgin olive oil
1 tablespoon finely shredded fresh basil

1 Combine spinach, capsicum, artichoke and olives in large bowl.
2 Place ingredients for lemon basil dressing in screw-top jar; shake well.
3 Cook mushroom on heated, oiled grill plate (or grill or barbecue), loosely covered with foil, about 5 minutes or until browned and tender, cover to keep warm.
4 Cook cheese, in batches, on grill plate until browned lightly both sides.
5 Top spinach mixture with mushroom, cheese and dressing.

grilled tuna with coriander dressing

preparation time 15 minutes
(plus refrigeration time)
cooking time 15 minutes

per serving 43.5g total fat
(7.8g saturated fat); 2767kJ
(662 cal); 20.5g carbohydrate;
44.2g protein; 5.9g fibre

tips The tuna is best marinated an
hour ahead. Recipe is best assembled
just before serving.

150g tuna steak
125g baby new potatoes
2 teaspoons olive oil
2 teaspoons lime juice
½ small red onion (50g), sliced thinly
1 tablespoon roasted pecans
50g baby spinach leaves
coriander dressing
½ teaspoon coriander seeds
1 clove garlic, peeled
¼ cup firmly packed fresh
   coriander leaves
1 tablespoon olive oil
2 teaspoons lime juice

1 Using mortar and pestle (or blender
or processor), pound ingredients for
coriander dressing until smooth. Rub
half the dressing over tuna; cover,
refrigerate 30 minutes.
2 Meanwhile, boil, steam or microwave
potatoes until tender; drain, slice thickly.
3 Cook tuna on heated, oiled barbecue
(or grill or grill plate) until cooked
as desired.
4 Combine remaining dressing with
oil and juice.
5 Combine potato, onion, nuts and
spinach; arrange on serving plate. Top
with tuna; drizzle with dressing mixture.

grilled prosciutto and asparagus salad

preparation time 10 minutes
cooking time 8 minutes

per serving 17.4g total fat
(5.4g saturated fat); 1070kJ
(256 cal); 3.7g carbohydrate;
19.7g protein; 3g fibre

60g thinly sliced prosciutto, halved
100g asparagus
30g rocket
60g yellow teardrop tomatoes, halved
1 tablespoon fresh basil leaves
2 teaspoons balsamic vinegar
2 teaspoons extra virgin olive oil
2 tablespoons parmesan cheese flakes

1 Wrap piece of prosciutto around two asparagus spears; secure with toothpicks. Repeat with remaining prosciutto and asparagus. Cook on heated, oiled barbecue (or grill or grill plate) until browned.
2 Meanwhile, arrange rocket, tomato and basil on serving plate.
3 Combine vinegar and oil in small jug.
4 Drizzle vegetables with dressing; top with cheese. Remove toothpicks from asparagus, serve with salad.

grilled vegetables with blue cheese polenta

preparation time 15 minutes
cooking time 10 minutes

per serving 19.2g total fat
(6.9g saturated fat); 1580kJ
(378 cal); 35.4g carbohydrate;
13.1g protein; 5.7g fibre

tips Vegetables can be prepared
several hours ahead. Polenta is
best made just before serving.

1 clove garlic, crushed
2 teaspoons olive oil
1 small zucchini (90g), sliced lengthways
1 finger eggplant (65g), quartered
   lengthways
½ medium red capsicum (100g),
   sliced thickly
½ cup (125ml) water
½ cup (125ml) vegetable stock
¼ cup (40g) polenta
25g blue cheese, crumbled
1 tablespoon coarsely chopped
   fresh chives

1 Combine garlic, oil and vegetables
in medium bowl; toss gently to coat
vegetables. Cook on heated grill pan
(or barbecue) until browned and tender.
2 Meanwhile, combine the water and
stock in medium saucepan; bring to
a boil. Reduce heat, simmer; gradually
whisk in polenta. Cook, stirring, about
5 minutes or until mixture is thick and
soft. Stir in cheese.
3 Serve polenta and char-grilled
vegetables sprinkled with chives.

veal cutlet with warm red lentils and cauliflower

preparation time 15 minutes
cooking time 20 minutes

per serving 23.5g total fat
(4g saturated fat); 2241kJ
(536 cal); 26.1g carbohydrate;
50g protein; 9.1g fibre

tip Serve with sautéed cauliflower, if desired.

¼ cup (50g) red lentils
1 tablespoon olive oil
½ small brown onion (40g), chopped finely
1 clove garlic, crushed
¼ cup (60ml) chicken stock
50g cherry tomatoes, halved
1 tablespoon black olives, coarsely chopped
2 tablespoons small fresh basil leaves
1 veal cutlet (200g)

1 Rinse lentils under cold water; drain. Heat oil in medium frying pan; cook onion and garlic, stirring, until onion is soft. Add lentils and stock, bring to a boil; reduce heat, simmer 10 minutes or until tender. Stir in tomato, olives and basil.
2 Meanwhile, cook cutlet in heated, oiled grill pan (or grill or barbecue) until cooked as desired. Remove from pan; cover, stand 5 minutes.
3 Serve cutlet on lentil mixture.

thai red curry lamb skewers

preparation time 10 minutes
cooking time 15 minutes

per serving 12.3g total fat
(4.4g saturated fat); 1074kJ
(257 cal); 7g carbohydrate;
28.2g protein; 2.2g fibre

tip Soak skewers in cold water for at
least an hour before using to prevent
them from splintering and scorching
during cooking.

2 teaspoons thai red curry paste
1 teaspoon fish sauce
1 teaspoon brown sugar
1 teaspoon lime juice
125g diced lamb
½ small red capsicum (75g),
   cut into 2cm pieces
2 lime wedges

1 Combine paste, sauce, sugar and juice
in small bowl.
2 Thread lamb and capsicum, alternately,
onto two skewers; thread one lime
wedge onto each skewer. Brush skewers
with half the curry paste mixture.
3 Cook skewers on heated, oiled grill
plate (or grill or barbecue), brushing
with remaining curry paste mixture
occasionally, until browned all over and
cooked as desired.

vegetarian frittata with potato

makes 2 servings
preparation time 10 minutes
cooking time 20 minutes

per serving 21.2g total fat
(6.7g saturated fat); 1643kJ
(393 cal); 23.3g carbohydrate;
25.3g protein; 3.9g fibre

tip Leftover frittata can be stored,
covered, in the refrigerator for up
to two days. Eat warm or cold with
a green salad, if desired.

300g baby new potatoes
2 teaspoons olive oil
1 small red capsicum (150g),
   chopped coarsely
½ small brown onion (40g),
   chopped finely
2 tablespoons coarsely chopped
   fresh basil
2 tablespoons coarsely chopped
   fresh flat-leaf parsley
5 eggs, beaten lightly
¼ cup (20g) grated parmesan cheese

1 Boil, steam or microwave potatoes
until tender; drain, cut into quarters.
2 Meanwhile, heat oil in small frying
pan; cook capsicum and onion, stirring,
until softened. Stir in potato.
3 Combine basil, parsley and egg; pour
into pan. Cook, over low heat, about
5 minutes or until edges are set.
4 Meanwhile, preheat grill.
5 Sprinkle top of frittata with cheese;
cook frittata under grill until browned
lightly and firm.

veal and eggplant parmigiana

preparation time 10 minutes
cooking time 20 minutes

per serving 20.3g total fat
(7.1g saturated fat); 1605kJ
(384 cal); 16.1g carbohydrate;
32.9g protein; 4.1g fibre

2 teaspoons olive oil
1 veal scaloppine (100g)
50g char-grilled eggplant
½ cup (125ml) bottled tomato
    pasta sauce
2 teaspoons fresh sage leaves
50g bocconcini cheese, sliced thinly

1 Heat oil in medium frying pan; cook veal until browned both sides. Remove pan from heat.
2 Top veal with eggplant, 1 tablespoon of the pasta sauce, sage and cheese. Spoon remaining sauce around veal.
3 Return pan to heat; simmer, covered, about 5 minutes or until sauce bubbles.
4 Meanwhile, preheat grill.
5 Place pan briefly under grill until cheese melts and browns lightly.

T-bone with blue-cheese butter and pear salad

preparation time 10 minutes
cooking time 10 minutes

per serving 66.8g total fat
(27.2g saturated fat); 3787kJ
(906 cal); 14.2g carbohydrate;
62.3g protein; 4.7g fibre

tip Refrigerate remaining butter
for another use, such as serving
over grilled chicken fillets.

1 beef T-bone steak (400g)
25g soft blue cheese
25g butter, softened
1 green onion, chopped finely
1 teaspoon wholegrain mustard
2 teaspoons olive oil
2 teaspoons red wine vinegar
25g mesclun
½ small pear (90g), sliced thinly
2 tablespoons roasted pecans

1 Cook beef on heated, oiled grill plate
(or grill or barbecue) until browned
both sides and cooked as desired.
2 Meanwhile, combine cheese, butter
and onion in small bowl.
3 Place mustard, oil and vinegar in
screw-top jar; shake well.
4 Place mesclun, pear and mustard
dressing in small bowl; toss gently to
combine. Sprinkle with nuts.
5 Spread half of the blue-cheese butter
on hot beef; serve with salad.

char-grilled salmon with avocado salsa

preparation time 10 minutes
cooking time 8 minutes

per serving 48.5g total fat
(9.2g saturated fat); 2613kJ
(625 cal); 4.7g carbohydrate;
41.9g protein; 2.2g fibre

200g salmon fillet
½ small avocado (100g), sliced thickly
½ small red onion (50g), sliced thinly
2 teaspoons chopped fresh dill
2 teaspoons drained baby capers, rinsed
25g rocket
lemon dressing
1 tablespoon lemon juice
1 tablespoon olive oil

1 Cook fish on lightly oiled grill plate
(or barbecue) until cooked as desired.
2 Meanwhile, combine avocado, onion,
dill and capers in medium bowl.
3 Place ingredients for lemon dressing
in screw-top jar; shake well.
4 Serve salmon with rocket and avocado
mixture; drizzle with dressing.

grilled lamb and capsicum with olive mash

preparation time 10 minutes
cooking time 15 minutes

per serving 39g total fat
(23.2g saturated fat); 2705kJ
(647 cal); 32.7g carbohydrate;
38.8g protein; 4.6g fibre

200g desiree potatoes,
   chopped coarsely
2 tablespoons cream
10g butter, chopped
1 tablespoon coarsely chopped
   black olives
½ small red capsicum (75g), quartered
2 lamb loin chops (200g)
2 tablespoons fresh mint leaves

1 Boil, steam or microwave potato until
tender; drain. Mash potato with cream
and butter in large bowl until smooth.
Stir in olives; cover to keep warm.
2 Meanwhile, cook capsicum and lamb
on heated grill plate (or grill or barbecue)
until capsicum softens and lamb is cooked
as desired.
3 Serve lamb with capsicum and olive
mash; sprinkle with mint.

lamb cutlets with char-grilled vegetable salad

preparation time 15 minutes
cooking time 10 minutes

per serving 41.4g total fat
(7.8g saturated fat); 2278kJ
(545 cal); 19.9g carbohydrate;
3.1g protein; 21.8g fibre

1 tablespoon olive oil
½ small kumara (125g), sliced thinly
3 lamb cutlets (150g)
50g marinated char-grilled eggplant,
    sliced thickly
50g marinated char-grilled capsicum,
    sliced thickly
50g char-grilled artichokes, quartered
½ cup loosely packed fresh
    flat-leaf parsley leaves
2 teaspoons balsamic vinegar

1 Combine half the oil with kumara in
small bowl. Cook kumara on heated,
oiled barbecue (or grill or grill pan)
until tender.
2 Cook lamb on heated, oiled barbecue
(or grill or grill pan) until browned on
both sides and cooked as desired.
3 Toss kumara, eggplant, capsicum,
artichoke and parsley in large bowl.
4 Serve vegetable mixture with lamb;
drizzle with combined vinegar and
remaining oil.

pork with celeriac and apple

preparation time 10 minutes
cooking time 15 minutes

per serving 16.7g total fat
(7.3g saturated fat); 1593kJ
(381 cal); 18.7g carbohydrate;
36g protein; 7.5g fibre

150g pork fillet
1 teaspoon olive oil
10g butter
¼ small celeriac (140g), peeled, cut
  into thin wedges
¼ small white onion (25g), sliced thinly
1 small apple (130g), sliced thinly
¼ teaspoon whole yellow mustard seeds
2 tablespoons chicken stock
1 teaspoon fresh sage leaves

1 Brush pork with oil; cook on heated
barbecue flat plate (grill or grill pan)
until cooked as desired. Remove from
heat; cover to keep warm.
2 Meanwhile, heat butter in small
saucepan; cook celeriac until browned
lightly. Add onion, apple and seeds;
cook, stirring, until onion is soft.
3 Add stock; cook, stirring, 3 minutes or
until celeriac and apple are just tender.
Remove from heat; stir in sage.
4 Slice pork thickly; serve with the
celeriac and apple mixture.

fillet steak with green capsicum salsa

preparation time 15 minutes
cooking time 15 minutes

per serving 9.3g total fat
(3.8g saturated fat); 1296kJ
(310 cal); 18.4g carbohydrate;
35.9g protein; 3.2g fibre

tips The salsa can be made several
hours ahead and kept, covered, in
the refrigerator.
Sirloin, scotch fillet or rump can be
substituted for the eye-fillet steaks.

3 baby new potatoes (120g), halved
1 beef eye-fillet steak (150g)
green capsicum salsa
½ small green capsicum (75g),
   chopped finely
¼ small red onion (25g), chopped finely
1 fresh small red thai chilli, seeded,
   chopped finely
2 teaspoons lime juice
1 tablespoon finely chopped fresh mint

1 Boil, steam or microwave potato until
tender; drain.
2 Meanwhile, combine ingredients for
green capsicum salsa in medium bowl.
3 Cook beef on heated, oiled grill plate
(or grill or barbecue) until browned both
sides and cooked as desired. Serve with
salsa and potato.

stir-fries & pan-fries

bacon-wrapped lamb chops with baby potatoes in olive pesto

preparation time 15 minutes
cooking time 20 minutes

per serving 5.2g total fat
(1.8g saturated fat); 911kJ
(218 cal); 27.5g carbohydrate;
12.5g protein; 4.5g fibre

tip Store remaining pesto, in single
portions, covered, in the freezer for
up to two months.

2 lamb loin chops (200g)
1 bacon rasher (70g), rind removed,
   halved lengthways
1 medium egg tomato (75g), halved
200g baby new potatoes, halved
olive pesto
2 tablespoons olive oil
1 cup firmly packed fresh basil leaves
1 tablespoon lemon juice
¼ cup (60ml) buttermilk
½ cup (60g) seeded green olives
¼ cup (40g) roasted pine nuts

1 Make olive pesto.
2 Wrap each chop around the outside
with one strip of bacon; securing each
with a toothpick.
3 Cook chops in heated, lightly oiled
medium frying pan until cooked as
desired. Remove toothpicks, cover
chops; stand 5 minutes.
4 Meanwhile, cook tomato in same pan,
cut-side down, until soft.
5 Boil, steam or microwave potato until
tender; drain.
6 Place potato and a quarter of the
pesto in large bowl; toss gently to
combine. Serve potato with chops and
tomato and, if desired, tomato chutney.
olive pesto Blend or process oil with
basil, juice and buttermilk until mixture
forms a smooth paste. Add olives and
nuts; process pesto until just combined.

pork and sage with fettuccine

preparation time 10 minutes
cooking time 15 minutes

per serving 19.1g total fat
(4.5g saturated fat); 2458kJ
(588 cal); 55.9g carbohydrate;
36g protein; 3.6g fibre

1 teaspoon olive oil
30g shaved ham
2 teaspoons fresh sage leaves
2 pork schnitzels (100g)
¼ cup (60ml) dry white wine
1 teaspoon brown sugar
75g fettuccine
30g baby spinach leaves
¼ small red onion (25g), sliced thinly
1 teaspoon olive oil, extra

1 Heat oil in medium frying pan; cook ham, stirring, until browned lightly. Remove from pan; cover to keep warm.
2 Cook sage in same pan, stirring, until just wilted. Remove from pan; cover to keep warm.
3 Cook pork in pan until cooked as desired. Remove from pan; cover to keep warm.
4 Combine wine and sugar in same pan; boil, uncovered, until sauce reduces by a third.
5 Meanwhile, cook pasta in medium saucepan of boiling water, uncovered, until just tender; drain.
6 Place pasta in medium bowl with spinach, onion and extra oil; toss gently to combine. Top pasta mixture with pork, ham and sage; drizzle with sauce.

veal paprika

preparation time 5 minutes
cooking time 10 minutes

per serving 27.5g total fat
(16.8g saturated fat); 1856kJ
(444 cal); 2.8g carbohydrate;
46.5g protein; 0.4g fibre

10g butter
2 veal schnitzels (200g)
pinch sweet paprika
1 teaspoon tomato paste
1 shallot (25g), chopped finely
2 tablespoons chicken stock
2 tablespoons sour cream

1 Melt butter in medium frying pan;
cook veal until cooked as desired.
Remove from pan; cover to keep warm.
2 Add paprika and paste to pan,
cook, stirring, 1 minute. Add shallot
and stock, bring to a boil; reduce heat,
simmer about 3 minutes or until sauce
is thickened slightly. Add sour cream;
stir until heated through.
3 Serve veal with sauce and, if desired,
mashed potato and a green salad.

spaghettini with parsley basil pesto

preparation time 10 minutes
cooking time 10 minutes

per serving 111g total fat
(22.1g saturated fat); 5961kJ
(1426 cal); 70.9g carbohydrate;
33.9g protein; 9.9g fibre

tip Store remaining pesto, in single
portions, covered, in the freezer for
up to two months.

100g spaghettini
1 cup firmly packed fresh basil leaves
1 cup firmly packed fresh flat-leaf
   parsley leaves
2 tablespoons roasted pine nuts
2 cloves garlic, quartered
2 tablespoons finely grated
pecorino cheese
⅓ cup (80ml) extra virgin olive oil
2 tablespoons finely grated pecorino
   cheese, extra

1 Cook pasta in medium saucepan
of boiling water, uncovered, until just
tender; drain.
2 Meanwhile, blend or process herbs,
nuts, garlic and cheese until combined.
With motor operating, gradually add oil
in a thin stream until combined.
3 Combine pasta with a quarter of the
pesto in medium saucepan; toss gently.
Serve sprinkled with extra cheese.

salmon in sesame crust

preparation time 10 minutes
cooking time 10 minutes

per serving 28.7g total fat
(5.3g saturated fat); 1919kJ
(459 cal); 2g carbohydrate;
46.9g protein; 2.3g fibre

tip You can also pound the seeds
and peppercorns using a mortar
and pestle, if preferred.

2 teaspoons sesame seeds
¼ teaspoon coriander seeds
¼ teaspoon black peppercorns
1 skinless salmon fillet (220g)
2 teaspoons sesame oil
¼ teaspoon grated fresh ginger
1 fresh small red thai chilli, seeded,
   sliced thinly lengthways
1 baby buk choy (120g),
   quartered lengthways
1 tablespoon soy sauce
2 teaspoons lime juice

1 Place seeds and peppercorns in strong plastic bag; crush with rolling pin or meat mallet. Coat one side of fish with seed mixture.
2 Heat half the oil in medium frying pan; cook fish, seeded-side down, 1 minute. Turn; cook until fish is cooked as desired. Remove from pan, cover to keep warm.
3 Heat remaining oil in pan; cook ginger and chilli until fragrant. Add remaining ingredients; cook, stirring, until buk choy just wilts.
4 Serve fish with buk choy, and steamed rice, if desired.

lamb burgers with beetroot and tzatziki

preparation time 10 minutes
cooking time 10 minutes

per serving 20.2g total fat
(7g saturated fat); 2926kJ
(700 cal); 78.7g carbohydrate;
45.8g protein; 6.6g fibre

tips The patties and yogurt mixture
can be made several hours ahead; keep
covered, in the refrigerator.
You can triple the pattie recipe to
make six patties. Store leftover patties,
wrapped individually in plastic wrap, in
the freezer for up to two months.

125g lamb mince
¼ small brown onion (20g),
  chopped finely
1 egg yolk
½ teaspoon grated lemon rind
2 tablespoons yogurt
¼ lebanese cucumber (30g), seeded,
  chopped finely
1 teaspoon chopped fresh mint
1 small turkish bread (160g)
½ cup shredded cos lettuce
¼ cup whole baby beetroot,
  drained, quartered

1 Combine lamb, onion, egg yolk and
rind in large bowl; mix well. Shape
mince mixture into two patties.
2 Cook patties in heated, oiled medium
frying pan, until cooked through.
3 Meanwhile, combine yogurt, cucumber
and mint in small bowl; mix well.
4 Preheat grill.
5 Cut bread in half horizontally, toast,
cut-side up, until browned lightly.
6 Just before serving, sandwich bread
with lettuce, patties, yogurt mixture
and beetroot.

pork schnitzel in lemon and parsley

preparation time 10 minutes
cooking time 15 minutes

per serving 22g total fat
(4.1g saturated fat); 2140kJ
(512 cal); 32.8g carbohydrate;
43.9g protein; 2.3g fibre

tip When crumbing pork steaks,
do some extra and freeze them,
individually wrapped, for up to
three months.

¼ cup (35g) stale breadcrumbs
2 teaspoons finely grated lemon rind
2 teaspoons finely chopped fresh
  flat-leaf parsley
1 pork leg steak (150g)
1 tablespoon plain flour
1 egg white
2 teaspoons milk
olive oil, for shallow-frying

1 Combine breadcrumbs, rind and parsley in medium bowl.
2 Toss pork in flour, shake away excess. Dip pork in combined egg and milk, then breadcrumb mixture; press on lightly.
3 Heat oil in large frying pan. Cook schnitzels, over medium heat, until browned both sides and just cooked through. Drain on absorbent paper.
4 Serve schnitzels with lemon wedges and steamed green beans, if desired.

chilli beef stir-fry

preparation time 20 minutes
cooking time 10 minutes

per serving 18.3g total fat
(4.9g saturated fat); 1584kJ
(379 cal); 16.2g carbohydrate;
35.9g protein; 4.9g fibre

1 long red chilli, sliced thinly
1cm piece fresh ginger (5g),
   chopped finely
2 shallots (25g), sliced thinly
1 tablespoon brown sugar
2 teaspoons vegetable oil
2 teaspoons fish sauce
150g beef strips
2 green onions, cut into 5cm lengths
100g gai lan, chopped coarsely
2 tablespoons fresh thai basil leaves

1 Blend or process chilli, ginger, shallot, sugar, oil and half the sauce until all ingredients are chopped finely.
2 Stir-fry chilli mixture in heated oiled wok about 5 minutes, stirring continuously, until fragrant and browned. Add beef, stir-fry 3 minutes.
3 Add onion and gai lan, stir-fry about 2 minutes or until gai lan is just wilted. Stir in remaining sauce and basil leaves.
4 Serve with steamed rice, if desired.

steamed fish with black bean and chilli sauce

preparation time 5 minutes
cooking time 8 minutes

per serving 7.9g total fat
(2g saturated fat); 1087kJ
(260 cal); 4.2g carbohydrate;
40.1g protein; 5.1g fibre

½ cup (125ml) water
125g gai lan, cut into 8cm lengths
1 snapper fillet (180g)
1cm piece fresh ginger (5g), sliced thinly
2 teaspoons black bean garlic sauce
1 teaspoon peanut oil
1 fresh small red thai chilli, seeded,
  sliced thinly

1 Bring water to a boil in medium frying pan; add stems of the gai lan, in single layer. Cook, covered tightly, for 1 minute.
2 Place gai lan leaves then fish and ginger on top of stems. Cook, covered tightly, about 5 minutes or until fish is just cooked through.
3 Meanwhile, heat sauce, oil and chilli in small saucepan, stirring, until hot.
4 Serve fish on gai lan; drizzle with sauce.

pan-fried tofu with cabbage salad

preparation time 15 minutes
cooking time 10 minutes

per serving 10.3g total fat
(1.5g saturated fat); 941kJ
(225 cal); 8.7g carbohydrate;
21.3g protein; 5.6g fibre

150g piece fresh firm silken tofu
1 fresh small red thai chilli, seeded,
  sliced thinly
½ small red onion (50g), sliced thinly
¼ cup (20g) bean sprouts
1 cup (80g) finely shredded wombok
2 tablespoons fresh coriander leaves
sweet and sour dressing
1 tablespoon lime juice
½ teaspoon grated palm sugar
2 teaspoons soy sauce

1 Pat tofu all over with absorbent paper;
slice thinly. Place tofu slices, in single layer,
on absorbent-paper-lined tray; cover
with more absorbent paper, stand at
least 10 minutes.
2 Meanwhile, combine ingredients for
sweet and sour dressing in small jug;
whisk until sugar dissolves.
3 Cook tofu in heated, lightly oiled large
frying pan until browned both sides.
4 Place remaining ingredients in large
bowl; toss gently to combine.
5 Place salad on serving plate; top with
tofu, serve with dressing.

lemon and ginger pork ribs with plum sauce

preparation time 30 minutes
cooking time 15 minutes
(plus cooling and refrigeration time)

per serving 14.3g total fat
(3.9g saturated fat); 1747kJ
(418 cal); 46.5g carbohydrate;
26.1g protein; 1.7g fibre

250g pork spare ribs
¼ cup (60ml) plum sauce
2 teaspoons soy sauce
½ teaspoon grated lemon rind
½ teaspoon grated fresh ginger
1 teaspoon peanut oil
50g snow peas, halved

1 Cut each rib section into three pieces;
place in medium saucepan. Cover with
cold water; bring to a boil. Drain; cool.
2 Combine ribs, sauces, rind and ginger
in medium bowl. Cover; refrigerate
3 hours or overnight.
3 Heat oil in wok; stir-fry undrained rib
mixture, in batches, until ribs are browned.
4 Return ribs to wok. Add snow peas;
stir-fry until hot.

chilli and garlic octopus

preparation time 10 minutes
(plus refrigeration time)
cooking time 5 minutes

per serving 23.2g total fat
(3.6g saturated fat); 2061kJ
(493 cal); 5.2g carbohydrate;
64.6g protein; 1.9g fibre

½ teaspoon coriander seeds, crushed
250g cleaned baby octopus
1 tablespoon olive oil
1 clove garlic, crushed
2 teaspoons lemon juice
2 teaspoons sweet chilli sauce
25g watercress, trimmed

1 Cook seeds in dry wok, stirring, about 1 minute or until fragrant.
2 Place seeds in large bowl with octopus, oil, garlic, juice and sauce; toss to combine. Cover; refrigerate 3 hours or overnight.
3 Cook drained octopus in heated oiled wok until cooked as desired. Gently toss octopus and watercress in medium bowl.

chinese omelette

makes 2 servings
preparation time 15 minutes
cooking time 10 minutes

per serving 36g total fat
(6g saturated fat); 1603kJ
(384 cal); 5g carbohydrate;
11.4g protein; 1g fibre

tip Cut the omelette in half, eat one
half for dinner and take the other
half to work for lunch the next day.

¼ small red capsicum (30g),
  sliced thinly
1 green onion, sliced thinly
¼ cup (20g) bean sprouts
30g fresh shiitake mushrooms,
  sliced thinly
2 tablespoons fresh coriander leaves
3 eggs
2 teaspoons fish sauce
½ teaspoon oyster sauce
¼ cup (60ml) vegetable oil
2 teaspoons oyster sauce, extra
¼ teaspoon sesame oil

1 Combine capsicum, onion, sprouts, mushroom and coriander in small bowl.
2 Combine eggs and sauces in medium bowl; beat lightly. Add half the vegetable mixture to egg mixture.
3 Heat vegetable oil in wok, stirring to coat sides. When oil is just smoking, add egg mixture, then, working quickly using a slotted spoon or wok chan, push the cooked egg mixture in from the sides of the wok (as for scrambled eggs) and the uncooked mixture to the outside.
4 When omelette is almost set, sprinkle remaining vegetables over one half of the omelette. Reduce heat to low; cook 1 minute, folding omelette in half over top of vegetables after 30 seconds. Remove omelette from wok with two lifters; drain on absorbent paper.
5 Combine extra oyster sauce and sesame oil in small bowl. If desired, top omelette with chives, extra coriander and green onions. Serve omelette with oyster sauce mixture.

hokkien noodle and lamb stir-fry

preparation time 10 minutes
cooking time 15 minutes

per serving 24.7g total fat
(8g saturated fat); 2624kJ
(867 cal); 108.4g carbohydrate;
49.3g protein; 5.5g fibre

tip Hokkien noodles are fresh
wheat noodles, also called shanghai
or stir-fry noodles. They're found in
the refrigerated section at the
supermarket. Store leftover noodles,
covered, in the refrigerator, for up to
one week.

150g hokkien noodles
150g lamb strips
2 teaspoons cornflour
¼ teaspoon salt
2 teaspoons peanut oil
½ small brown onion (40g),
   sliced thickly
1cm piece fresh ginger (5g), grated
½ small red capsicum (75g),
   sliced thinly
50g snow peas, trimmed, halved
1 tablespoon plum sauce
1 tablespoon oyster sauce
1 tablespoon water

1 Place noodles in medium heatproof
bowl, cover with hot water; separate
noodles with fork, drain.
2 Place lamb in medium bowl with
cornflour and salt; toss lamb to coat
in mixture.
3 Heat half the oil in wok; stir-fry lamb,
in batches, until browned all over.
4 Heat remaining oil in wok; stir-fry
onion and ginger until onion softens.
Add capsicum and snow peas; stir-fry
until just tender. Return lamb to wok
with noodles, sauces and the water;
stir-fry until heated through.

garlic and chilli prawns

preparation time 10 minutes
cooking time 8 minutes

per serving 19.2g total fat
(2.7g saturated fat); 1258kJ
(301 cal); 0.5g carbohydrate;
31.2g protein; 1.1g fibre

300g uncooked king prawns
1 tablespoon extra virgin olive oil
1 clove garlic, sliced thinly
1 fresh small red thai chilli, seeded,
    chopped finely
2 tablespoons coarsely chopped
    fresh flat-leaf parsley
½ teaspoon finely grated lemon rind

1 Shell and devein prawns, leaving
tails intact. Cut along backs of prawns,
taking care not to cut all the way
through; flatten prawns slightly.
2 Heat oil in large frying pan, add
prawns; cook until almost cooked
through. Add garlic and chilli; cook
about 2 minutes or until fragrant and
prawns are just cooked through.
3 Remove from heat, stir in parsley
and lemon rind.
4 Serve prawns with lemon wedges
and crusty bread, if desired.

chicken and gai lan stir-fry

preparation time 10 minutes
cooking time 15 minutes

per serving 22.1g total fat
(6.7g saturated fat); 2513kJ
(602 cal); 36.1g carbohydrate;
57.3g protein; 13.9g fibre

tip Any type of fresh noodle
can be used in this recipe.

125g fresh singapore noodles
2 teaspoons peanut oil
200g chicken tenderloins, halved
½ small brown onion (40g),
    sliced thickly
1 clove garlic, crushed
250g gai lan, chopped coarsely
1 tablespoon oyster sauce
1 teaspoon light soy sauce

1 Place noodles in medium heatproof
bowl, cover with boiling water; separate
noodles with fork, drain.
2 Heat half the oil in wok; stir-fry chicken,
in batches, until cooked through.
3 Heat remaining oil in wok; stir-fry
onion and garlic until onion softens.
4 Return chicken to wok with gai lan and
sauces; stir-fry until gai lan just wilts. Toss
chicken mixture with noodles to serve.

soy duck breast with noodles

preparation time 15 minutes
(plus refrigeration time)
cooking time 10 minutes

per serving 17.5g total fat
(6.9g saturated fat); 2098kJ
(502 cal); 38.7g carbohydrate;
36.7g protein; 10.1g fibre

tips Duck breast can be marinated
a day ahead.
Store any leftover noodles, covered,
in the refrigerator, for up to one week.

1 duck breast fillet (150g)
1 tablespoon chinese cooking wine
1 tablespoon soy sauce
2 teaspoons finely grated fresh ginger
1 teaspoon white sugar
1 fresh small red thai chilli, seeded,
  chopped finely
¼ bunch gai lan (150g),
  chopped coarsely
150g thin fresh hokkien noodles

1 Score skin and fat of duck breast
through to the flesh. Place duck in
small bowl with combined wine,
sauce, ginger, sugar and chilli. Cover,
refrigerate 1 hour. Drain duck from
marinade; reserve marinade.
2 Cook duck, skin-side down, in
heated lightly oiled small frying pan,
about 6 minutes or until skin is
browned and crisp. Turn duck, cook
3 minutes or until cooked as desired.
Cover duck, stand 5 minutes.
3 Meanwhile, boil, steam or microwave
gai lan until just tender, drain.
4 Place reserved marinade in same pan;
bring to a boil. Reduce heat, simmer,
uncovered, 1 minute.
5 Place noodles in medium heatproof
bowl, cover with boiling water; stand
2 minutes, separate noodles with fork.
Drain noodles.
6 Serve duck with noodles and gai lan;
drizzle with hot marinade.

pork larb

preparation time 10 minutes
cooking time 20 minutes

per serving 26g total fat
(8.7g saturated fat); 2136kJ
(511 cal); 3.4g carbohydrate;
63.1g protein; 3.5g fibre

tip Larb is a classic thai salad that can be made with beef, chicken or pork mince, vegetables or tofu.

1 teaspoon peanut oil
2 teaspoons finely chopped fresh
   lemon grass
½ fresh small red thai chilli, seeded,
   chopped finely
1 clove garlic, crushed
1cm piece fresh ginger (5g), grated
300g pork mince
2 teaspoons fish sauce
2 tablespoons lime juice
1 fresh kaffir lime leaf, shredded finely
2 tablespoons coarsely chopped
   fresh mint
2 tablespoons fresh coriander leaves
1 shallot (25g), sliced thinly
2 large iceberg lettuce leaves

1 Heat oil in large frying pan, add lemon grass, chilli, garlic and ginger; cook, stirring, until fragrant.
2 Add pork; cook, stirring, until cooked through. Add sauce and half the juice; cook, stirring, 5 minutes. Transfer mixture to medium bowl; stir in lime leaf, herbs, shallot and remaining juice.
3 Place two lettuce leaves together to form a "bowl" on serving plate; top with larb.

chicken and almond stir-fry

preparation time 10 minutes
cooking time 15 minutes

per serving 36.9g total fat
(4.3g saturated fat); 2629kJ
(629 cal); 14.7g carbohydrate;
56.2g protein; 8.1g fibre

tip You can use cashews instead
of almonds, if preferred.

¼ cup (40g) blanched whole almonds
2 teaspoons peanut oil
200g chicken breast fillets, sliced thinly
½ small red onion (50g),
   chopped coarsely
1 clove garlic, crushed
2 teaspoons hoisin sauce
50g green beans, trimmed, halved
½ trimmed celery stalk (50g),
   sliced thinly
1 teaspoon light soy sauce
1 teaspoon plum sauce

1 Heat wok; stir-fry almonds until
browned lightly, remove from wok.
2 Heat half the oil in wok; stir-fry
chicken, in batches, until browned all
over and cooked through.
3 Heat remaining oil in wok; stir-fry
onion and garlic until fragrant. Add
hoisin sauce, beans and celery; stir-fry
until beans are just tender.
4 Return chicken to wok with remaining
sauces; stir-fry until heated through. Toss
almonds through chicken mixture.

mussels with white wine and vegetables

preparation time 10 minutes
cooking time 15 minutes

per serving 16.8g total fat
(6.9g saturated fat); 1885kJ
(451 cal); 46g carbohydrate;
20g protein; 5g fibre

500g small blue mussels
10g butter
½ small brown onion (40g),
   chopped finely
½ small carrot (35), chopped finely
½ trimmed celery stalk (50g),
   chopped finely
½ clove garlic, crushed
2 tablespoons dry white wine
2 slices crusty bread
1 teaspoon olive oil
2 tablespoons coarsely chopped
   fresh flat-leaf parsley

1 Scrub mussels; remove beards.
2 Heat butter in medium saucepan,
add onion, carrot, celery and garlic;
cook, stirring, until onion is soft.
3 Add wine, bring to a boil. Add mussels;
cook, covered, about 5 minutes or until
mussels open (discard any that do not).
4 Meanwhile preheat grill.
5 Brush bread with oil; toast both sides
under grill until browned lightly.
6 Sprinkle mussels and broth with
parsley; serve with toast.

cook now
for later

oven-braised lamb shanks

makes 3 servings
preparation time 10 minutes
cooking time 3 hours and 25 minutes

per serving 25.4g total fat
(11.5g saturated fat); 2437kJ
(583 cal); 14.7g carbohydrate;
60.8g protein; 6.2g fibre

tip Reserve lamb braising liquid
(including carrot, celery and onion)
for following recipes, page 84-85.

6 french-trimmed lamb shanks (1.5kg)
3 cloves garlic, quartered
1 medium carrot (120g),
    chopped coarsely
2 trimmed celery stalks (200g),
    chopped coarsely
2 medium onions (300g),
    chopped coarsely
¾ cup (180ml) white wine
1½ cups (375ml) chicken stock
400g can tomato puree
3 bay leaves
6 sprigs fresh thyme

1 Preheat oven to 240°C/ 220°C
fan-forced.
2 Pierce meatiest part of each shank
in two places with a sharp knife; press
garlic into cuts.
3 Layer carrot, celery, onion and shanks
in large flameproof baking dish. Cook
15 minutes; turn shanks, cook a further
10 minutes. Remove dish from oven.
4 Reduce oven temperature to
160°C/140°C fan-forced.
5 Pour over combined wine, stock and
puree; add bay leaves and thyme. Cover
dish tightly with a double thickness of
foil; cook 1½ hours. Turn shanks; cook
further 1½ hours or until tender.
Remove bay leaves and thyme.
6 Serve two lamb shanks with mashed
potato and steamed green beans,
if desired.

3 WAYS WITH LAMB SHANKS

This dish forms the basis of a 3-in-1 recipe – make this
recipe now, and use the remaining portions as part of
the following two recipes to eat during the week.

pappardelle with lamb and eggplant ragù

makes 1 serving
preparation time 10 minutes
cooking time 20 minutes

per serving 15.6g total fat
(5.1g saturated fat); 2851kJ
(682 cal); 86.4g carbohydrate;
36.2g protein; 11.4g fibre

tip Fettuccine can be used instead
of the pappardelle, if preferred.

2 cooked lamb shanks (see *oven-braised lamb shanks* recipe, page 82)
1 teaspoon olive oil
2 baby eggplants (120g), sliced thickly
1 clove garlic, crushed
½ cup (125ml) braising sauce (see *oven-braised lamb shanks* recipe, page 82)
¼ cup (60ml) chicken stock
1 teaspoon balsamic vinegar
2 tablespoons green olives
100g dried pappardelle pasta
¼ cup coarsely chopped fresh flat-leaf parsley

1 Remove meat from lamb shanks and shred coarsely.
2 Heat oil in large frying pan; cook eggplant until browned both sides, remove from pan.
3 Add garlic to pan; cook, stirring, until fragrant, but not browned. Add lamb, braising liquid and stock. Bring to a boil; reduce heat, simmer about 5 minutes or until mixture has thickened slightly. Stir in vinegar and olives.
4 Meanwhile, cook pasta in medium pan of boiling water until just tender. Drain.
5 Add pasta, eggplant and parsley to lamb mixture, toss to combine.

lamb and barley broth

makes 1 serving
preparation time 10 minutes
cooking time 30 minutes

per serving 31.9g total fat
(12.7g saturated fat); 3423kJ
(819 cal); 47.9g carbohydrate;
67.4g protein; 13.5g fibre

1 teaspoon olive oil
1 clove garlic, crushed
¼ cup (50g) pearl barley
1½ cups (375ml) water
½ cup (125ml) chicken stock
2 cups (500ml) braising sauce
    (see *oven-braised lamb shanks*
    recipe, page 82)
2 cooked lamb shanks (see *oven-braised
    lamb shanks* recipe, page 82),
    coarsely shredded
¼ cup chopped fresh flat-leaf parsley
1 tablespoon lemon juice

1 Heat oil in large saucepan; cook garlic and barley 2 minutes, stirring continuously. Add the water and stock. Bring to a boil; reduce heat, simmer, covered, about 30 minutes or until barley is tender.
2 Add braising sauce, lamb, parsley and juice; cook, stirring, until heated through.

chicken with tomatoes and green olives

makes 4 servings
preparation time 10 minutes
cooking time 30 minutes

per serving 27.9g total fat
(7.6g saturated fat); 2241kJ
(536 cal); 14.1g carbohydrate;
49.7g protein; 4.8g fibre

tip Serve one portion now and
freeze the remainder, in single
portions, for up to three months.

1 tablespoon olive oil
4 chicken thighs (880g)
4 chicken drumsticks (600g)
½ cup (125ml) dry white wine
8 cloves garlic, peeled
1 tablespoon finely chopped
   fresh lemon thyme
3 bay leaves
100g semi-dried tomatoes
1½ cups (375ml) chicken stock
2 teaspoons cornflour
1 tablespoon water
⅓ cup (50g) seeded green olives

1 Heat oil in large heavy-based frying
pan, add chicken; cook until browned
lightly all over.
2 Add wine to pan; bring to a boil.
Add garlic, thyme, bay leaves, tomatoes
and stock; simmer, covered, about
5 minutes or until chicken is cooked
through. Remove chicken from pan;
cover to keep warm.
3 Add blended cornflour and water
to pan; stir until mixture boils and
thickens slightly.
4 Return chicken to pan with olives;
simmer until heated through. Discard
bay leaves before serving with mashed
potato, if desired.

sausages with borlotti beans

makes 4 servings
preparation time 15 minutes
cooking time 25 minutes

per serving 51.1g total fat
(22.8g saturated fat); 2884kJ
(690 cal); 27g carbohydrate;
29.1g protein; 9.5g fibre

tip Serve one portion now and freeze
the remainder, in single portions, for
up to three months.

1 tablespoon olive oil
8 thick Italian sausages
1 large brown onion (200g),
  chopped finely
3 cloves garlic, crushed
400g can chopped tomatoes
400g can borlotti beans,
  rinsed, drained
1 cup (250ml) beef stock
1 cup (250ml) water
2 tablespoons coarsely chopped
  fresh flat-leaf parsley

1 Heat the oil in large frying pan; cook sausages until well browned all over. Remove from pan; cool slightly then slice thickly.
2 Cook sausage pieces on cut surfaces until browned; remove from pan and drain on absorbent paper. Drain all but 1 tablespoon of the fat from the pan.
3 Cook onion and garlic in same pan until onion is soft. Add undrained tomatoes, beans, stock and the water. Return sausages to pan; simmer, uncovered, about 10 minutes or until mixture thickens slightly.
4 Sprinkle sausage mixture with parsley; serve with mashed potato, if desired.

corned beef

makes 3 servings
preparation time 10 minutes
cooking time 1 hour 10 minutes
(plus standing time)

per serving 16.3g total fat
(7.5g saturated fat); 1877kJ
(449 cal); 11.9g carbohydrate;
62.6g protein; 1.7g fibre

tip Reserve the corned beef poaching
liquid for recipe on page 93.

750kg piece corned silverside
1 bay leaf
2 tablespoons malt vinegar
2 tablespoons brown sugar
½ teaspoon black peppercorns
1 small carrot (70g), chopped coarsely
1 small onion (80g), halved
1 trimmed celery stalk (100g),
   chopped coarsely

1 Place beef in large saucepan with bay
leaf, vinegar, sugar, peppercorns, carrot,
onion and celery. Cover completely
with cold water; bring to a boil. Reduce
heat, simmer, covered, 1 hour or until
tender. Remove from heat, stand
30 minutes.
2 Remove beef from poaching liquid,
cover to keep warm. Strain liquid into
a large jug; reserve poaching liquid for
recipe, page 93. Discard vegetables.
3 Serve one third of the corned beef,
warm or cold, with coleslaw and crusty
bread, if desired.

3 WAYS WITH CORNED BEEF

This dish forms the basis of a 3-in-1 recipe – make this
recipe now, and use the remaining portions as part of
the following two recipes to eat during the week.

corned beef hash with poached egg

makes 1 serving
preparation time 15 minutes
cooking time 15 minutes

per serving 51.2g total fat
(10.2g saturated fat); 2738kJ
(655 cal); 17.2g carbohydrate;
30.5g protein; 3g fibre

2 cooked baby new potatoes (80g)
100g cooked corned beef (see *corned beef* recipe, page 91), shredded finely
½ small carrot (35g), grated coarsely
1 green onion, sliced thinly
1 egg yolk
2 teaspoons plain flour
2 tablespoons olive oil
1 tablespoon white vinegar
1 egg, extra
1 green onion, sliced thinly, extra

1 Coarsely grate unpeeled potatoes. Combine potato with corned beef in medium bowl; add carrot, onion, egg yolk and flour. Shape mixture into two patties.

2 Heat oil in large frying pan; cook patties over medium heat until browned both sides, turning carefully as mixture is quite loose. Drain corned beef hash on absorbent paper; cover to keep warm.

3 Meanwhile, bring 10cm of water to a boil in deep frying pan with the vinegar. Crack egg into cup. Pour egg carefully into the water. Lower heat to a gentle simmer; cook egg, uncovered, about 4 minutes or until cooked as desired. Remove egg using slotted spoon; drain on absorbent paper.

4 Serve egg on top of hash. Sprinkle with extra chopped green onion, and serve with rocket leaves, if desired.

corned beef with mustard sauce

makes 1 serving
preparation time 15 minutes.
cooking time 20 minutes

per serving 33.4g total fat
(19.2g saturated fat); 3553kJ
(850 cal); 70g carbohydrate;
61.7g protein; 10.5g fibre

reserved corned beef poaching liquid
(see *corned beef* recipe, page 91)
4 baby new potatoes (160g)
3 baby carrots (60g)
10g butter, softened
1 tablespoon finely chopped fresh
flat-leaf parsley
200g cooked corned beef (see *corned
beef* recipe, page 91), sliced thinly
mustard sauce
10g butter
2 teaspoons plain flour
½ cup (125ml) milk, warmed
1 teaspoon dijon mustard

1 Place reserved liquid in medium
saucepan, bring to a boil. Add potatoes,
simmer, uncovered, about 10 minutes.
Add carrots, simmer, uncovered, until
carrots and potatoes are tender; drain.
2 Meanwhile, make mustard sauce.
3 Place potatoes in small bowl with
butter and parsley. Toss gently to combine.
4 Place corned beef on microwave-safe
plate. Reheat in microwave oven on
HIGH (100%) about 30 seconds or until
warm. Serve warm corned beef with
mustard sauce, potatoes and carrots.
mustard sauce Melt butter in small
saucepan, add flour; cook, stirring, about
1 minute. Stir in milk; cook, stirring, until
sauce boils and thickens. Stir in mustard.

beef and red wine casserole

makes 6 servings
preparation time 20 minutes.
cooking time 2 hours 20 minutes

per serving 15.4g total fat
(4.8g saturated fat); 1471kJ
(352 cal); 7.3g carbohydrate;
43.1g protein; 1.2g fibre

tip Serve one portion now and freeze
the remainder, in single portions, for
up to three months.

1.2kg beef chuck steak, diced into
  2cm cubes
2 tablespoons plain flour
2 tablespoons olive oil
400g pickling onions, halved
1 clove garlic, crushed
⅓ cup (80ml) dry red wine
2⅓ cups (580ml) beef stock
1 tablespoon tomato paste
1 bay leaf
2 sprigs fresh thyme

1 Toss beef in flour; shake away excess.
Heat oil in large saucepan; cook beef, in
batches, until well browned.
2 Add onion and garlic to pan; cook,
stirring, 5 minutes. Add wine; simmer,
uncovered, until mixture is reduced by
half. Add stock, tomato paste and beef;
bring to a boil then reduce heat.
3 Add bay leaf and thyme; simmer,
covered, 1 hour, stirring occasionally.
Simmer, uncovered, for further 1 hour
or until tender and thickened. Remove
bay leaf and thyme.
4 Serve with mashed potato, if desired.

red lentil and vegetable stew

makes 4 servings
preparation time 25 minutes
cooking time 45 minutes

per serving 12.1g total fat
(1.7g saturated fat); 1597kJ
(382 cal); 37.7g carbohydrate;
20.4g protein; 16.7g fibre

tip Serve one portion now and freeze
the remainder, in single portions, for
up to three months.

4 medium zucchini (480g)
4 baby eggplants (240g)
1 medium red capsicum (200g)
2 tablespoons olive oil
2 cloves garlic, crushed
1 medium leek (350g), sliced thinly
1 teaspoon caraway seeds
1 teaspoon cumin seeds
2 x 400g cans chopped tomatoes
⅓ cup (80ml) dry red wine
1 teaspoon brown sugar
¼ cup (60ml) tomato paste
1 cup (200g) red lentils
2 cups (500ml) vegetable stock
1 tablespoon finely chopped
   fresh basil

1 Halve zucchini and eggplants
lengthways. Quarter capsicum,
remove seeds and membranes.
2 Heat 1 tablespoon of the oil on
grill plate; cook vegetables, in batches,
until browned on both sides, remove.
3 Heat remaining oil in large saucepan;
cook garlic, leek and seeds, stirring, until
leek is soft. Add undrained tomatoes,
wine, sugar, tomato paste and lentils;
simmer, uncovered, 5 minutes.
4 Stir in stock, basil and grilled vegetables;
simmer, uncovered, about 15 minutes or
until vegetables are tender.

roast chicken with lemon and garlic

makes 3 servings
preparation time 25 minutes
cooking time 40 minutes

per serving 37.9g total fat
(13.7g saturated fat); 2157kJ
(516 cal); 1.5g carbohydrate;
40.7g protein; 2.4g fibre

tip Reserve roasted garlic and lemon
for recipe on page 101.

1.2kg chicken
20g butter, softened
6 cloves garlic, unpeeled
1 medium lemon (140g)
2 tablespoons coarsely chopped
   fresh flat-leaf parsley
2 teaspoons sea salt flakes

1 Preheat oven to 220°C/200°C
fan-forced).
2 Wash chicken under cold water; pat
dry with absorbent paper. Using kitchen
scissors, cut along both sides of chicken
backbone; discard backbone. Cut thigh
and leg portions from chicken; cut wing
portions from chicken. Using knife, slice
breast from either side of breastbone;
discard breastbone. You will now have
eight pieces.
3 Rub chicken pieces with butter.
Refrigerate chicken breasts. Place thighs,
wings and drumsticks, skin-side up, in oiled,
heavy-based baking dish; place a garlic
clove under each piece. Roast 15 minutes.
4 Meanwhile, using a zester, remove
rind from the lemon; cut lemon into
six wedges. Combine rind, parsley and
salt in small bowl.
5 Place chicken breasts, skin-side down,
in same baking dish with other chicken
pieces; roast 10 minutes. Turn chicken
breasts over, brush chicken with pan juices.
6 Add lemon wedges; sprinkle chicken
with rind mixture; roast for a further
15 minutes or until chicken is browned
and cooked through.
7 Serve chicken thighs with roasted
vegetables of your choice.

3 WAYS WITH ROAST CHICKEN

This dish forms the basis of a 3-in-1 recipe – make this
recipe now, and use the remaining portions as part of
the following two recipes to eat during the week.

moroccan-style chicken with buttered couscous

makes 1 serving
preparation time 15 minutes
cooking time 20 minutes

per serving 64.4g total fat
(25.5g saturated fat); 4226kJ
(1011 cal); 58.7g carbohydrate;
47g protein; 5.1g fibre

tip Lemon rind can be substituted for
the preserved lemon rind, if desired.

5g butter
½ teaspoon ground coriander
½ teaspoon ground cumin
¼ teaspoon sweet paprika

2 roasted chicken drumsticks
    (see *roasted chicken with lemon
    and garlic* recipe, page 98)
¼ cup (60ml) chicken stock
2 tablespoons seeded green
    olives, halved
1 teaspoon finely chopped preserved
    lemon rind
1 tablespoon roasted slivered almonds
1 tablespoon coarsely chopped
    fresh coriander
buttered couscous
¼ cup (60ml) chicken stock
¼ cup (60ml) water
20g butter, chopped
⅓ cup (65g) couscous

1 Heat butter in medium frying pan;
cook spices, stirring, until fragrant. Add
chicken; turn to coat in spice mixture.
Add stock; cook, covered, about 5 minutes
or until chicken is heated through.
2 Meanwhile, make couscous.
3 Add olives, lemon and nuts to
chicken mixture; stir until heated
through. Serve chicken mixture with
buttered couscous; top with coriander.
buttered couscous Bring stock, the
water and half the butter to a boil in
small saucepan. Pour stock mixture
over couscous in medium heatproof
bowl; stand, covered, 3 minutes. Add
remaining butter, fluff couscous with fork.

chicken breasts with carrot puree

makes 1 serving
preparation time 10 minutes
cooking time 10 minutes

per serving 64.6g total fat
(28g saturated fat); 3804kJ
(910 cal); 18.4g carbohydrate;
56.7g protein; 11.9g fibre

2 medium carrots (240g),
    chopped coarsely
½ cup (125ml) chicken stock
¾ cup (180ml) water
2 roasted chicken breasts
    (see *roasted chicken with lemon
    and garlic* recipe, page 98)
1 clove roasted garlic, peeled
    (see *roasted chicken with lemon
    and garlic* recipe, page 98)
10g butter
1 tablespoon thickened cream
roasted lemon wedges, for serving
    (see *roasted chicken with lemon
    and garlic* recipe, page 98)

1 Combine carrot, stock and the water in medium saucepan; bring to a boil. Reduce heat; simmer about 10 minutes or until carrot is tender. Drain; reserve 2 tablespoons of the cooking liquid.
2 Meanwhile, place chicken breasts on microwave-safe plate. Reheat chicken in microwave oven on HIGH (100%) for 1 minute or until heated through.
3 Blend or process carrot, garlic, butter, cream and reserved cooking liquid until smooth.
4 Serve carrot puree with chicken breasts, lemon wedges and steamed broccolini, if desired.

apple, pork and prune casserole

makes 4 servings
preparation time 25 minutes
cooking time 1 hour 30 minutes

per serving 47.1g total fat
(14.2g saturated fat); 3854kJ
(922 cal); 55.1g carbohydrate;
68.2g protein; 5.8g fibre

tip Serve one portion now and freeze
the remainder, in single portions, for
up to three months.

2 tablespoons vegetable oil
2 small leeks (400g), sliced thinly
4 forequarter pork chops (1.75kg)
1 tablespoon plain flour
1 litre (4 cups) chicken stock
½ cup (100g) long-grain rice
4 medium apples (600g), sliced thickly
1 cup (170g) seeded prunes
2 tablespoons coarsely chopped
   fresh sage

1 Heat one-third of the oil in 2.5 litre
(10-cup) flameproof casserole dish; cook
leek, stirring, until soft. Remove from dish.
2 Preheat oven to 180°C/160°C
fan-forced.
3 Trim fat and bone from chops; cut
pork into 5cm pieces. Toss pork in
flour; shake away excess.
4 Heat remaining oil in dish; cook pork,
stirring, until browned. Add leek and
stock; cook, covered, in oven 45 minutes.
5 Remove dish from oven; skim off any
fat. Stir in rice, apple, prunes and half
the sage; cook, covered, about 20 minutes
or until pork is tender.
6 Serve sprinkled with remaining sage.

chilli con carne

makes 4 servings
preparation time 25 minutes
cooking time 1 hour 30 minutes

per serving 18.5g total fat
(4.9g saturated fat); 1777kJ
(425 cal); 17.2g carbohydrate;
43.9g protein; 6.6g fibre

tip Serve one portion now and freeze
the remainder, in single portions, for
up to three months.

750g beef chuck steak
2 tablespoons olive oil
2 small brown onions (160g),
　chopped finely
2 cloves garlic, crushed
2 teaspoons ground cumin
1 teaspoon ground coriander
1 teaspoon chilli powder
1 tablespoon finely chopped
　fresh oregano
2 x 400g cans chopped tomatoes
½ cup (125ml) beef stock
2 teaspoons brown sugar
310g can red kidney beans,
　rinsed, drained

1 Cut beef into 2cm pieces. Heat half
the oil in large saucepan; cook beef, in
batches, until browned. Drain on
absorbent paper.
2 Heat remaining oil in pan; cook onion,
garlic, spices and oregano, stirring, until
onion is soft.
3 Add undrained tomatoes, stock, sugar
and beef; simmer, covered, about 1 hour
or until beef is tender.
4 Stir beans into beef mixture; simmer
5 minutes or until heated through.

fruit desserts

pear with coffee syrup

preparation time 15 minutes
cooking time 15 minutes

per serving 8.1g total fat
(5.2g saturated fat); 1292kJ
(309 cal); 57.7g carbohydrate;
2.7g protein; 2.8g fibre

1 medium pear (125g)
2 tablespoons white sugar
½ cup (125ml) water
¼ teaspoon instant coffee granules
1 square dark eating chocolate
1 scoop vanilla ice-cream

1 Peel pear, cut in half crossways.
2 Combine sugar and the water in
small saucepan; stir over medium heat
until the sugar is dissolved. Add pear;
simmer, covered, about 10 minutes or
until pear is tender. Remove from syrup.
3 Add coffee to syrup; stir until dissolved.
Serve pear with coffee syrup, chocolate
and ice-cream.

honey grilled plums and figs

preparation time 5 minutes
cooking time 8 minutes

per serving 3.4g total fat
(1.9g saturated fat); 1104kJ
(264 cal); 51.1g carbohydrate;
4.7g protein; 5.2g fibre

2 small plums (150g), halved, seeded
2 medium figs (140g), halved
1 tablespoon honey
2 teaspoons brown sugar
2 tablespoons thick Greek-style yogurt

1 Preheat grill.
2 Place plums and figs on shallow
baking tray. Drizzle with half the honey,
sprinkle with sugar. Place under grill
until browned lightly and just tender.
3 Serve fruit, drizzled with remaining
honey, pan juices and yogurt.

rhubarb and muesli parfait

preparation time 10 minutes
cooking time 5 minutes

per serving 2.8g total fat
(1.4g saturated fat); 435kJ
(104 cal); 16g carbohydrate;
2.7g protein; 1.9g fibre

1 cup (110g) coarsely chopped rhubarb
2 tablespoons brown sugar
⅓ cup (95g) thick Greek-style yogurt
⅓ cup (45g) toasted muesli

1 Combine rhubarb and sugar, in single layer, in medium, shallow microwave-safe dish. Cook, covered, on HIGH (100%) about 3 minutes or until just tender; drain if necessary. Cool.
2 Serve rhubarb, topped with yogurt and muesli.

apple and brown sugar crumble

preparation time 10 minutes.
cooking time 30 minutes.

per serving 16.9g total fat
(10.9g saturated fat); 1605kJ
(384 cal); 54.4g carbohydrate;
3.3g protein; 4.5g fibre

tip We used Granny Smith apples in
this recipe.

2 small apples (260g), coarsely chopped
2 teaspoons lemon juice
1 teaspoon brown sugar
¼ teaspoon mixed spice
2 tablespoons plain flour
20g butter, chopped
1 tablespoon brown sugar, extra

1 Preheat oven to 200°C/180°C
fan-forced. Lightly grease 1-cup (250ml)
ovenproof dish; place on oven tray.
2 Combine apple, juice, sugar and
half the spice in medium bowl.
3 Place remaining spice and flour in
another medium bowl; rub in butter until
combined. Add extra sugar; mix well.
4 Spoon apple mixture into dish; press
crumble mixture over top of apples.
Bake about 30 minutes or until browned.
5 Serve hot with ice-cream or cream,
if desired.

mixed melon salad with lime syrup

preparation time 15 minutes
cooking time 5 minutes

per serving 0.8g total fat
(0g saturated fat); 648kJ
(155 cal); 33.5g carbohydrate;
2g protein; 3.3g fibre

200g watermelon
200g rockmelon
200g honeydew melon
lime syrup
1 tablespoon brown sugar
½ teaspoon finely grated lime rind
2 teaspoons lime juice
1 tablespoon water

1 Combine ingredients for lime syrup in small saucepan. Stir over low heat until sugar dissolves. Cool.
2 Remove skin and seeds from melons, cut into chunks. Combine melons with syrup in large bowl; toss to coat in syrup.

blackberry clafoutis

preparation time 10 minutes
cooking time 25 minutes

per serving 23.5g total fat
(13.6g saturated fat); 1751kJ
(419 cal); 44.7g carbohydrate;
2.2g protein; 8.9g fibre

1 teaspoon caster sugar
¼ cup (35g) frozen blackberries
1 tablespoon milk
2 tablespoons cream
¼ teaspoon vanilla extract
1 egg
2 tablespoons caster sugar, extra
1 teaspoon plain flour

1 Preheat oven to 180°C/160°C
fan-forced. Grease shallow ¾-cup
(180ml) ovenproof dish; sprinkle
inside of dish with caster sugar. Place
blackberries in dish.
2 Bring milk, cream and extract to a boil
in small saucepan. Remove from heat.
3 Whisk egg and extra sugar in small
bowl until creamy. Whisk flour and
strained milk mixture into egg mixture.
Pour over blackberries.
4 Place dish on oven tray. Bake about
20 minutes or until browned and set.
5 Dust with sifted icing sugar, if desired.

grilled nectarines and passionfruit yogurt

makes 3 servings
preparation time 10 minutes.
cooking time 10 minutes

per serving 2.7g total fat
(1.5g saturated fat); 1062kJ
(254 cal); 41.7g carbohydrate;
6.6g protein; 7.3g fibre

tips Store leftover servings, covered, in
the refrigerator for up to three days.
Nectarines and yogurt are great served
with muesli for breakfast.

6 medium nectarines (1kg),
  halved, seeded
2 tablespoons brown sugar
1 tablespoon Grand Marnier or
  orange juice
¾ cup (210g) natural yogurt
1 tablespoon icing sugar
2 tablespoons passionfruit pulp

1 Preheat grill.
2 Place nectarines, cut-side up, on
baking tray; sprinkle with sugar and
liqueur. Grill nectarines until browned.
3 Meanwhile, combine yogurt and icing
sugar in medium bowl, spoon into serving
bowl, swirl with passionfruit pulp.
4 Serve nectarines with passionfruit yogurt.

balsamic strawberries with crème fraîche

preparation time 10 minutes
(plus standing time)

per serving 8.1g total fat
(5.3g saturated fat); 623kJ
(149 cal); 15g carbohydrate;
2.6g protein; 2.8g fibre

tip Replace crème fraîche with yogurt
or thick cream, if desired.

125g strawberries, quartered
2 teaspoons balsamic vinegar
1 tablespoon icing sugar
1 tablespoon crème fraîche

1 Combine strawberries, vinegar and
icing sugar in a bowl. Stand 30 minutes.
2 Serve strawberry mixture topped
with crème fraîche.

glossary

ARTICHOKE HEARTS tender centre of the globe artichoke; purchased in cans or glass jars.

BACON RASHERS also known as bacon slices.

BASIL, THAI also known as horapa; has smallish leaves and sweet licorice/aniseed taste. Available from Asian food stores and supermarkets.

BEANS
green these long fresh beans are also known as french or string beans.
red kidney medium-sized red bean, with a slightly floury, yet sweet, flavour; sold dried or canned.
sprouts also known as bean shoots.

BEETROOT also known as red beets.

BREADCRUMBS
packaged fine-textured, crunchy, purchased white breadcrumbs.
stale one- or two-day-old bread made into crumbs by blending or processing.

BUK CHOY also called chinese white cabbage or pak choy; has a fresh, mild mustard taste. *Baby buk choy is slightly more tender than buk choy.*

BUTTER use salted or unsalted (sweet) butter; one stick of butter equals 125g.

BUTTERMILK sold alongside fresh milk products in supermarkets; despite the implication of its name, it is low in fat.

CAPERS the grey-green buds of a warm climate (usually Mediterranean) shrub, sold either dried and salted or pickled in brine. Rinse well before using.

CAPSICUM also known as bell pepper or, simply, pepper. Can be red, green, yellow, orange or purplish black. Discard seeds and membranes before use.

CELERIAC tuberous root with brown skin, white flesh and a celery-like flavour.

CHEESE
blue mould-treated cheeses mottled with blue veining.
bocconcini a fresh, delicate, semi-soft, white, walnut-sized baby mozzarella.

fetta a crumbly goat- or sheep-milk cheese with a sharp, salty taste.
haloumi a firm, cream-coloured sheep-milk cheese matured in brine; can be fried, briefly, without breaking down.
parmesan also known as parmigiano; a hard, grainy cows-milk cheese.
pecorino the generic Italian name for cheeses made from sheep milk.
pizza a commercial blend of grated mozzarella, cheddar and parmesan.
swiss generic name for a variety of cheeses originating in Switzerland.

CHILLI
Use rubber gloves when seeding and chopping fresh chillies as they can burn your skin. Removing seeds and membranes lessens the heat level.
red thai also known as "scuds"; tiny, very hot and bright red in colour.

CHINESE COOKING WINE also known as hao hsing or chinese rice wine; made from fermented rice, wheat, sugar and salt. Found in Asian food shops; if you can't find it, replace with mirin or sherry.

CRÈME FRAÎCHE mature fermented cream having a tangy, nutty flavour.

CORIANDER also known as cilantro or chinese parsley; bright-green leafy herb with a pungent flavour.

CORNFLOUR also known as cornstarch.

CUCUMBER, LEBANESE short, slender and thin-skinned, with tiny, yielding seeds and a sweet, fresh taste.

CUMIN also known as zeera.

EGGS some recipes in this book may call for raw or barely cooked eggs; exercise caution if there is a salmonella problem in your area.

FETTUCCINE ribbon pasta available fresh or dried.

FLOUR
plain all-purpose flour made from wheat.
self-raising plain flour sifted with baking powder in the proportion of 1 cup flour to 2 teaspoons baking powder.

FOCACCIA a flat Italian-style bread.

GAI LAN also known as gai larn, chinese broccoli, gai lum and chinese kale; this vegetable is prized more for its stems than its coarse leaves.

GINGER also known as green or root ginger; the thick root of a tropical plant. Ground ginger cannot be substituted.

GNOCCHI, FRESH Italian "dumplings" made of potatoes, semolina or flour.

HORSERADISH
cream a creamy prepared paste of grated horseradish, vinegar, oil and sugar.
prepared grated horseradish with flavourings; do not confuse with horseradish cream.

KAFFIR LIME LEAVES also known as bai magrood; sold fresh, dried or frozen. Looks like two glossy dark green leaves joined end to end, forming a rounded hourglass shape. A strip of fresh lime peel may be substituted for each kaffir lime leaf.

KUMARA orange-fleshed sweet potato often confused with yam.

LEMON GRASS a tall, clumping, lemon-smelling and -tasting, sharp-edged grass; the white lower part of each stem is chopped and used in Asian cooking.

LEMON, PRESERVED salted lemons preserved in a mixture of olive oil and lemon juice are a North African specialty usually added to casseroles and tagines to impart a rich, salty-sour acidic flavour. Available from good food shops and delicatessens. Rinse well under cold water before using.

LENTILS (red, brown, yellow) dried pulses often identified by, and named after, their colour.

LETTUCE
cos also known as romaine lettuce.
iceberg a heavy, firm, round lettuce with tightly packed leaves and crisp texture.
radicchio a member of the chicory family; has dark burgundy leaves and a strong bitter flavour.

rocket also known as arugula, rugula and rucola; a peppery-tasting green leaf.

MESCLUN a salad mix of assorted young lettuce and green leaves, including baby spinach, mizuna and curly endive.

MINCE also known as ground meat.

MIXED SPICE a blend of ground spices including cinnamon, allspice and nutmeg.

MUSHROOMS

portobello mature swiss browns. Large, dark brown mushrooms with full-bodied flavour; ideal for filling or barbecuing.

shiitake when fresh are also known as chinese black, forest or golden oak mushrooms. Are large and meaty; often used as a substitute for meat in some Asian vegetarian dishes. When dried, are known as donko or dried chinese mushrooms; rehydrate before use.

NOODLES

fresh egg also known as yellow noodles; Range in size from very fine strands to wide, thick spaghetti-like pieces.

hokkien also known as stir-fry noodles; fresh wheat noodles resembling thick, yellow-brown spaghetti.

OIL

olive made from ripened olives. *Extra virgin* and *virgin* are the first and second press of the olives, while *extra light* or *light* refers to taste, not fat levels.

peanut pressed from ground peanuts; has a high smoke point (the capacity to handle high heat without burning).

sesame made from roasted, crushed, white sesame seeds; a flavouring rather than a cooking medium.

vegetable sourced from plants rather than animal fats.

ONIONS

green also known as scallion or, incorrectly, shallot; an immature onion picked before the bulb has formed, having a long, bright-green edible stalk.

red also known as spanish, red spanish or bermuda onion; a sweet-flavoured, large, purple-red onion that is particularly good eaten in raw salads.

shallots also called french shallots, golden shallots or eschalots; small, brown-skinned, elongated members of the onion family.

PAPPARDELLE wide pasta with rippled sides.

PAPRIKA ground dried red capsicum (bell pepper), available sweet or hot.

PARSLEY, FLAT-LEAF also known as continental or italian parsley.

PINE NUTS also known as pignoli; not, in fact, a nut, but a small, cream-coloured kernel from pine cones.

PITTA also known as lebanese bread. This pocket bread is sold in large, flat pieces that separate into two thin rounds. Also available in small thick pieces called pocket pitta.

POLENTA also known as cornmeal; a flour-like cereal made of dried corn (maize); also the name of the dish made from it.

PROSCIUTTO cured, air-dried (unsmoked), pressed ham.

SAUCES

black bean a chinese sauce made from fermented soy beans, spices, water and wheat flour.

cranberry made of cranberries cooked in sugar syrup; its astringent flavour goes well with roast poultry and meats.

fish made from pulverised salted fermented fish (most often anchovies); has a pungent smell and strong taste.

hoisin a thick, sweet and spicy chinese paste made from salted fermented soy beans, onions and garlic.

oyster Asian in origin, this rich, brown sauce is made from oysters and their brine, cooked with salt and soy sauce, and thickened with starches.

pasta a prepared tomato-based sauce (sometimes called ragu or sugo on the label); comes in varying degrees of thickness and kinds of spicing.

plum a thick, sweet and sour dipping sauce made from plums, vinegar, sugar, chillies and spices.

soy also known as sieu; made from fermented soy beans.

worcestershire thin, dark-brown spicy sauce used as a seasoning for meat and gravies and as a condiment.

SPINACH also known as english spinach and, incorrectly, silver beet.

SUGAR

brown a soft, fine granulated sugar retaining molasses for its characteristic colour and flavour.

caster also known as superfine or finely granulated table sugar.

icing sugar also known as powered or confectioners' sugar; granulated sugar crushed together with a small amount of cornflour.

palm sugar also known as nam tan pip, jaggery, jawa or gula melaka; made from the sap of the sugar palm tree. Light brown to black in colour and usually sold in rock-hard cakes; substitute with brown sugar, if unavailable.

white coarse, granulated table sugar, also known as crystal sugar.

TANDOORI PASTE consisting of garlic, tamarind, ginger, coriander, chilli and spices.

TOFU (tao hu) also known as bean curd; an off-white, custard-like product made from the "milk" of crushed soy beans. Comes fresh as soft or firm, and processed as fried or pressed dried sheets. Refrigerate leftover fresh tofu in water (which is changed daily) for up to four days.

TURKISH BREAD also known as pide. Comes in long (about 45cm) flat loaves as well as individual rounds.

VANILLA EXTRACT vanilla beans that have been submerged in alcohol. Vanilla essence is not a suitable substitute.

VIETNAMESE MINT not a mint at all, but a pungent and peppery narrow-leafed member of the buckwheat family.

WOMBOK also known as peking, napa or chinese cabbage, wong bok or petsai. Elongated with pale green, crinkly leaves.

conversion chart

MEASURES

One Australian metric measuring cup holds approximately 250ml; one Australian metric tablespoon holds 20ml; one Australian metric teaspoon holds 5ml.

The difference between one country's measuring cups and another's is within a two- or three-teaspoon variance, and will not affect your cooking results. North America, New Zealand and the United Kingdom use a 15ml tablespoon.

All cup and spoon measurements are level. The most accurate way of measuring dry ingredients is to weigh them. When measuring liquids, use a clear glass or plastic jug with the metric markings.

We use large eggs with an average weight of 60g.

DRY MEASURES

METRIC	IMPERIAL
15g	½oz
30g	1oz
60g	2oz
90g	3oz
125g	4oz (¼lb)
155g	5oz
185g	6oz
220g	7oz
250g	8oz (½lb)
280g	9oz
315g	10oz
345g	11oz
375g	12oz (¾lb)
410g	13oz
440g	14oz
470g	15oz
500g	16oz (1lb)
750g	24oz (1½lb)
1kg	32oz (2lb)

LIQUID MEASURES

METRIC	IMPERIAL
30ml	1 fluid oz
60ml	2 fluid oz
100ml	3 fluid oz
125ml	4 fluid oz
150ml	5 fluid oz (¼ pint/1 gill)
190ml	6 fluid oz
250ml	8 fluid oz
300ml	10 fluid oz (½ pint)
500ml	16 fluid oz
600ml	20 fluid oz (1 pint)
1000ml (1 litre)	1¾ pints

LENGTH MEASURES

METRIC	IMPERIAL
3mm	⅛in
6mm	¼in
1cm	½in
2cm	¾in
2.5cm	1in
5cm	2in
6cm	2½in
8cm	3in
10cm	4in
13cm	5in
15cm	6in
18cm	7in
20cm	8in
23cm	9in
25cm	10in
28cm	11in
30cm	12in (1ft)

OVEN TEMPERATURES

These oven temperatures are only a guide for conventional ovens.
For fan-forced ovens, check the manufacturer's manual.

	°C (CELSIUS)	°F (FAHRENHEIT)	GAS MARK
Very slow	120	250	½
Slow	150	275-300	1-2
Moderately slow	160	325	3
Moderate	180	350-375	4-5
Moderately hot	200	400	6
Hot	220	425-450	7-8
Very hot	240	475	9

index

ARE YOU MISSING SOME OF THE WORLD'S FAVOURITE COOKBOOKS?

The Australian Women's Weekly Cookbooks are available from bookshops, cookshops, supermarkets and other stores all over the world. You can also buy direct from the publisher, using the order form below.

TITLE	RRP	QTY	TITLE	RRP	QTY
Asian Meals in Minutes	£6.99		Japanese Cooking Class	£6.99	
Babies & Toddlers Good Food	£6.99		Just For One	£6.99	
Barbecue Meals In Minutes	£6.99		Kids' Birthday Cakes	£6.99	
Beginners Cooking Class	£6.99		Kids Cooking	£6.99	
Beginners Simple Meals	£6.99		Kids' Cooking Step-by-Step	£6.99	
Beginners Thai	£6.99		Lean Food	£6.99	
Best Food	£6.99		Low-carb Low-fat	£6.99	
Best Food Desserts	£6.99		Low-fat Feasts	£6.99	
Best Food Fast	£6.99		Low-fat Food For Life	£6.99	
Best Food Mains	£6.99		Low-fat Meals in Minutes	£6.99	
Cafe Classics	£6.99		Main Course Salads	£6.99	
Cakes Biscuits & Slices	£6.99		Mexican	£6.99	
Cakes Cooking Class	£6.99		Middle Eastern Cooking Class	£6.99	
Caribbean Cooking	£6.99		Midweek Meals in Minutes	£6.99	
Casseroles	£6.99		Moroccan & the Foods of North Africa	£6.99	
Casseroles & Slow-Cooked Classics	£6.99		Muffins, Scones & Breads	£6.99	
Cheesecakes: baked and chilled	£6.99		New Casseroles	£6.99	
Chicken	£6.99		New Classics	£6.99	
Chicken Meals in Minutes	£6.99		New Curries	£6.99	
Chinese Cooking Class	£6.99		New Finger Food	£6.99	
Christmas Cooking	£6.99		New Salads	£6.99	
Chocolate	£6.99		Party Food and Drink	£6.99	
Cocktails	£6.99		Pasta Meals in Minutes	£6.99	
Cooking for Friends	£6.99		Potatoes	£6.99	
Cupcakes & Fairycakes	£6.99		Salads: Simple, Fast & Fresh	£6.99	
Detox	£6.99		Saucery	£6.99	
Dinner Beef	£6.99		Sauces Salsas & Dressings	£6.99	
Dinner Lamb	£6.99		Sensational Stir-fries	£6.99	
Dinner Seafood	£6.99		Slim	£6.99	
Easy Curry	£6.99		Stir-fry	£6.99	
Easy Spanish-Style	£6.99		Superfoods for Exam Success	£6.99	
Foods That Fight Back	£6.99		Sweet Old-fashioned Favourites	£6.99	
Essential Soup	£6.99		Tapas Mezze Antipasto & other bites	£6.99	
French Food, New	£6.99		Thai Cooking Class	£6.99	
Fresh Food for Babies & Toddlers	£6.99		Traditional Italian	£6.99	
Good Food Fast	£6.99		Vegetarian Meals in Minutes	£6.99	
Great Lamb Cookbook	£6.99		Vegie Food	£6.99	
Greek Cooking Class	£6.99		Wicked Sweet Indulgences	£6.99	
Grills	£6.99		Wok Meals in Minutes	£6.99	
Healthy Heart Cookbook	£6.99				
Indian Cooking Class	£6.99		TOTAL COST:	£	

Mr/Mrs/Ms _____

Address _____

_____ Postcode _____

Day time phone _____ Email* (optional) _____

I enclose my cheque/money order for £ _____

or please charge £ _____

to my: ☐ Access ☐ Mastercard ☐ Visa ☐ Diners Club

PLEASE NOTE: WE DO NOT ACCEPT SWITCH OR ELECTRON CARDS

Card number ☐☐☐☐ ☐☐☐☐ ☐☐☐☐ ☐☐☐☐

Expiry date _____ 3 digit security code *(found on reverse of card)* _____

Cardholder's name_____ Signature _____

To order: Mail or fax – photocopy or complete the order form above, and send your credit card details or cheque payable to: Australian Consolidated Press (UK), Moulton Park Business Centre, Red House Road, Moulton Park, Northampton NN3 6AQ, phone (+44) (0) 1604 497531 fax (+44) (0) 1604 497533, e-mail books@acpuk.com or order online at www.acpuk.com

Non-UK residents: We accept the credit cards listed on the coupon, or cheques, drafts or International Money Orders payable in sterling and drawn on a UK bank. Credit card charges are at the exchange rate current at the time of payment.

Postage and packing UK: Add £1.00 per order plus 50p per book.

Postage and packing overseas: Add £2.00 per order plus £1.00 per book.

All pricing current at time of going to press and subject to change/availability.

Offer ends 31.12.2007

* By including your email address, you consent to receipt of any email regarding this magazine, and other emails which inform you of ACP's other publications, products, services and events, and to promote third party goods and services you may be interested in.

International Terrorism

ISSUES

Volume 212

Series Editor

Lisa Firth

 Independence

Educational Publishers
Cambridge

First published by Independence

The Studio, High Green

Great Shelford

Cambridge CB22 5EG

England

© Independence 2011

British Library Cataloguing in Publication Data

International terrorism. -- (Issues ; v. 212)

1. Terrorism. 2. Terrorism--Prevention.

I. Series II. Firth, Lisa.

363.3'25-dc23

ISBN-13: 978 1 86168 592 6

Printed in Great Britain

MWL Print Group Ltd